T0132032

To order additional copies of this book, contact:
Xlibris
844-714-8691
www.Xlibris.com
Orders@Xlibris.com

ISBN: Softcover   978-1-6641-3153-8
        EBook   978-1-6641-3152-1

Print information available on the last page

Rev. date: 09/21/2020

Wear

It

Where?

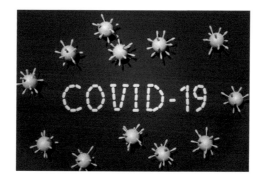

I will not
wear it

while I eat

I will not wear it

on my feet

I will not wear it

as I drink from a jar

I will not wear it

driving in my car

I will not wear it
if you stay away

I will not wear
it during my

alone
time
today

I will not wear it

here or there

I will not wear it

Everywhere

But if you crowd my

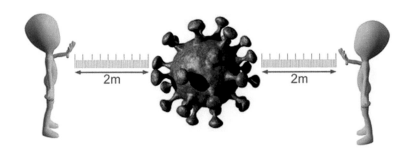

six-foot space

I will proudly wear it

upon my face

SAFETY FIRST

To keep me safe and you as well

What is this thing please do tell?

A mask that covers up

my face

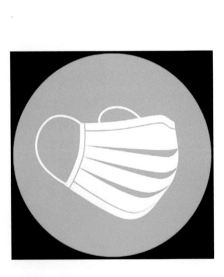

A mask that keeps

Coronavirus away

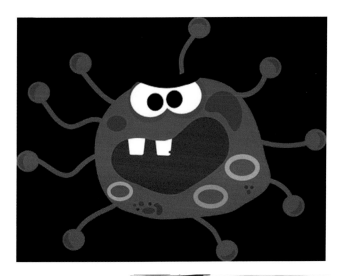

For now, we must diligently do this task:

BE DILIGENT

mask

task

But soon I will gladly

trash this mask!!

THANK YOU TO ALL FIRST RESPONDERS AND FRONT-LINE WORKERS FOR YOUR DEDICATION AND PERSERVERANCE DURING THE COVID-19 PANDEMIC

About the Author

Tom Robinson was born March 8, 1964 in Wilmington, N.C. He found his passion in life to be the fire service to which many hours have been committed in the past thirty years. For nine years this service came as a volunteer firefighter, and then it became a career path in his professional life. Many life experiences throughout his career led him to find poetry as an outlet to express feelings and emotions not normally shared in this profession. Tom attended Coastal Carolina Community College in Jacksonville, N.C. and is a graduate of Columbia Southern University in Alabama. Tom received a bachelor's degree in Fire Protection/Occupational Safety. Tom is currently an Assistant Chief in the fire service. Tom does have one work that has been recognized in the wake of 9-11. "In Remembrance" became the official poem for the Remembrance Flag and copies of this poem are sent with each flag purchased. Life is for experiencing and poetry allows those experiences to be expressed.

This book came to me sitting on the couch wondering when this pandemic might be over. The thought of a helpful chuckle towards a very serious situation led me to put this in a format that I believe all ages can enjoy and get a little smile from. Every day find at least one thing that brings a smile and if you have trouble finding that one thing maybe this book will bring that smile, we all need. We are in this together.